NEVER COMING HOME

TYLER VILE

Library of Congress Cataloging-in-Publication Data is available.

ISBN 978-1-62729-014-2 -- (paperback)

10 9 8 7 6 5 4 3 2 1
Cover design by Chloe Batch
Author photo by Faith Bocian

For Jamie, my sister

CONTENTS

NEVER
COMING HOME

TYLER VILE

I.

CHILDHOOD: SLEEP

When I dream the house burns down
all the paintings in it come
out unscathed, but everything else
smells like turpentine, the wool,
the wood, the leather couch, the
television. The hardwood floor
is kindling a kiln for every sculpture
in the living room.

It's all burning:
old braces,
white tennis shoes,
empty cereal boxes,
the ironing board we
eat dinner off of,
the vacations we take
when the water isn't running,
the car as we drive away,
my head on Jamie's
shoulder, the front seats
where Bob and Pam
aren't talking again.

We're stuck in traffic
on the Verrazano
when I wake up,
the fire is a headlight,
heading the other way.

SISTER: GONE

I'm going to college soon, Ty,
It's just gonna be you, mom,
and dad, okay? You take
care of mom, cuz god knows
dad won't. He'll yell at you,
but he won't actually help.

Let's face it, I've been
more of a mother to
you than she has,
which is fucked up.

Stop laughing, it's actually
fucked up. You don't know
how hard it is to take care
of you. You can't even
tie your shoes, kid,
what are you gonna do
when you're older?

Look, don't cry,
don't call me
too often,
be strong, ok?

MOTHER: SISTER

That ungrateful cunt has
no right to say she's
a better mother than me,
she has no idea what it's
like to be a mother.

I put your fucking shoes on
for you every morning, I cook
you breakfast, I take you to school,
I drive you to physical therapy and
listen to you whine about it,
what more do you want from me?

You love Jamie so much?
She hates you, you're
always in her way.

She doesn't forgive you
for pulling the nose off
her sculpture while the
clay was still wet.

I bet she is so glad to be rid of you,
I would be, that's for damn sure.

HOME: SISTER

My doubles partner's
daughter didn't get
into RISD, and the
poor girl offed herself.

Her parents put too much
stress on her. I don't see
how you can do that to a
kid, it's just not right.

I'm proud of Jamie for getting
into RISD, but I still think
it's stupid of her not to go
to MICA. What's the idea,
costing me money,
leaving us behind?

You don't wanna go to an
out of state college when
you're older, do you?

Good, you'll always be close to home.

CRIPS: WHEELCHAIR SPORTS

I.
I hate being in a wheelchair,
it makes me feel so small,
even when I'm in a room
full of other kids in wheelchairs.

II.
Maybe I can show you
some cool stuff so you'll
like it better. I could
teach you to do a wheelie.

III.
I know how to do a wheelie, idiot.
I don't have to get around this
way, I can walk, I'm less
affected than you are, so shut up.

IV.
Maybe you can walk a little,
but you still suck at everything.
You don't even like swimming.
What's wrong, you afraid of the water?

V.
I do like the water and
I don't suck at swimming.
If you fall, you float,
it's so easy.
I'm gonna go to
the ocean and swim
the fuck away.

HOME: BLUE ROOM BLUES

I'm staring out the window
as turkey vultures circle
a dead deer on our lawn.

They're tearing at every tendon
and I'm wishing it was my blood
browning in the melting snow.

I'm not a stranger to responsibility:
I'm going to try to hang myself
from that stupid little pear tree.

Will it take my weight?
Maybe I'll just grab a pillow
and suffocate and die.

One wall the color of ocean,
one wall the color of sky.

CHILDHOOD: BUILDING

I.
I want to build a bigger
house, design it myself,
make it accessible for Tyler,
give Jamie her own art studio.

I been building for those
rich pricks so long,
It's time I made
something for my family.

II.
I just got laid off, Bob,
I really don't want to start
doing this now, it'd be too
much for me and the kids.

III.
If anything, we'll
make money from it.
It'll be like having a
walk-in portfolio
for my clients. Then, when
we're ready, we'll sell it.

IV.
Let's wait a few years,
maybe until Jamie's
out of high school.

V.
Why wait?
Let's do it now!
We need a bigger
space and this is
my dream, Pam,
I've waited my
whole life for this.

VI.
Why would you care what I think?
My father warned me this would
happen if I married a kike.
Fuck it, I guess we're doing it.

VII.
That's what I like to hear.
you could even get a real
estate license, you've always
been good at sales.

VIII.
These tests are too hard, Bob,
I've been studying for months,
I don't know if I want my license

anymore, I want to figure out
something else.

IX.
Oh, bullshit,
what are you, stupid?
I could pass these tests!
You're just not trying.

X.
I am trying, asshole,
You try taking care
of a pain in the ass
disabled kid
and having low
blood sugars all the time,
not just losing clients and tennis matches.

XI.
Don't talk that way to me,
you stupid bitch, I've never
lost a client and you know it.

XII.
What about the
Feldmans or the
Goldbergs, or my
old boss, Dr. Frankel?

He won't even call me now
because of you. Stop building
this house, you're gonna dig us
deeper into debt than we already are.

XIII.
You want me to stop now?
I can't, the drywall guy's coming
on Wednesday, the electrician's
coming on Thursday,
and the hardwood floor guy
was supposed to come
on Friday, but he cancelled.

XIV.
Fucking cancel them all.
I don't care, I don't want
this anymore; I never did.
You never listen.

XV.
I never listen?
how about you listen to me?
I just told you we can't stop,
it's too late for that.

We gotta be outta the old house
by next week, but we won't
have occupancy for another

three months or so.
It could be a long wait
for running water.

XVI.
Fuck you, Bob.
I'm sick of your shit,

I'm going to go live
with my brother
in Texas.

XVII.
Is that a joke?
I'm not laughing, Pam.

Who's gonna test your blood,
Tyler? Who's the hospital
gonna call when you're
at death's door? Me,
that's who. Cut the shit.

XVIII.
I guess you're right,
I'm sorry I said that,
I love you.

AUNT: BABY BROTHER

Bobby, I didn't know you moved
to Egypt, you're living in the land
of De Nile. I'm serious, buddy, if
you don't get your shit together,
you're gonna lose your kids, your
wife, and your big stupid house.

Daddy told you not to build
this thing. He said it right before
he died, remember? "Live within
your means." What are you doing,
trying to impress our rich cousins?
It ain't workin', kid, they all make
fun of you behind your back.

You know how they got rich?
They married into it. So, you
don't get all the fancy things
you want, big deal, you should
be happy with your family.

I don't care how mean Pam is
to you, you don't fucking hit her
in front of your kid.
Grow up, Bobby, it's not all about you.

CHILDHOOD: TESTING KIT

Grab mom's finger,
press the middle
until the tip's red,
take the needle,

put it against the
ball of the tip and
push the button,
you'll hear a click.

wipe her finger
with a tissue
and--oh, look,
the reader's
beeping,

can you tell me
what that number
is? Right. 17,
she's very low.

If she gets below
10 and you're
alone, call 911.

Ty, what do you
need right now?
I'm too fucking tired.

Yeah, I know,
bad word,
deal with it.

CHILDHOOD: PIKESVILLE GIANT

Some lady said, "Oh, honey,
my heart goes out to you!"
I kept on going.
Dragging my walker
down the frozen foods aisle.
Mom was passed out
in the produce section.

A Jewish grandmother who wore
make-up to cover her Alzheimer's,
laughed as I fell face-first
by the checkout counter,

the cashier yanked me up
by the shoulders, I grabbed
onto him, almost shook him,
said, "Thanks, I don't have
money on me, but we need
to get my mother orange juice."

SISTER: PROVIDENCE

This hill's too steep,
Jamie, help, I'm
gonna fall!

It's not bleeding, is it?
How much longer is
the walk to your place?

My arms and legs are
tired, my knees are
kinda shaky, can we
rest for a minute?

I wanna go to that
record store, oh,
and that hot dog
place before I leave.

Aren't you glad
that after this
we get to take a road trip
with Jackie for a week?

AUNT: NEW ENGLAND

There's Mars right next to
the moon, it's so red, I wish
I could see it every night.

Thank you for taking me here
to see the pilgrim village and
that guy–what's his name–
Thoreau's house at Walden Pond,
I wanna be like him, live where nobody
could bother you, but do you think
he'd be happy to see all those people
swimming in that pond?

Tomorrow, are we going to
Lexington and Concord?
I learned in class that nobody
said, "The British are coming,"
they said, "the redcoats are coming,"
because the colonists grew up
calling themselves British and–
do you think there will ever be
another revolution, Aunt Jackie?
I think we need one.

What about you, Jamie,
do you think we need a revolution?
Let's start our own,
the three of us!

Jackie, what if you never
had to take me back to
Mom and Dad's and I
lived with you in
New York, we could
come visit Jamie in
Providence and do
this every summer.
Wouldn't that be great?

CHILDHOOD: BEDTIME STORIES

Do you want to hear a story about when I was a little girl?
There was this tornado when your uncle and I were
    younger,
he ran outside, a tree trunk missed his head by an
inch. I said to him, "Get back inside you stupid shit,
    you'll kill yourself."

That was the only time he ever listened to me,
You know, he hit me over the head with a telephone
    receiver once
when I told him to get off the phone.
It was heavy back in those days, it was lead, and he just
    went WHACK!
He knocked me unconscious, the bastard.

Do you want to hear another story?
When I was about your age, I came home and the floor
    was a mess
with broken glass, green glass, brown glass, all kinds of
    glass. I'm telling you,
I have never seen more glass in my life. Your grandma
    and grandpa were
threatening to rip each other's throats out with the end
    of a bottle, I laughed my
ass off, so they started throwing them at me, both of
    them, it was the first thing
I'd seen them do together besides drink and argue.

You have it so good, honey, you don't even know,
daddy and I don't really drink, we're nothing like that,
Will you make me feel better, sweetie?
Suck on mommy's titty, okay?

Some people would say
You're too old to still be sucking my breasts,
but it feels nice, and I'm your mother.

I'll always have my baby, won't I?
Yes I will. You'll never leave me.
If you ever left me I think I'd kill myself.
Now, give mommy a kiss goodnight.

MOTHER: HOME

Damn right I want to divorce,
but I don't know if I can
last long on my own, you'll
take care of me, won't you?

Doesn't your dad understand
that it's harder for me
to make a living?
Fuck him and his house.

I didn't mean to say that,
it's a beautiful house,
he did a great job
designing it, it's just
too much sometimes,
you know?

We're in so much debt
I want to cry. Sometimes
I think about killing him,
don't you dare ever tell
him I said that, got it?

That's between you and me.
You don't say that when he
picks you up from school today,
okay? Now, get out of the car.

HOME: MOTHER

That bitch wants a divorce,
I can't fucking believe it,
doesn't she know she'd
be living in a trailer park,
dead in a week without me?

Idiot. She doesn't appreciate
this house, she doesn't appreciate
me. Stupid, lazy, vindictive
bitch. All women are like that
deep down, you find a pretty one
you think you love and one
day you wake up next to a witch.

She was so nice and sweet
before we got married.
Don't ever let that happen
to your wife.
Your mother and I love
each other very much; we're
never getting divorced.

You tell that bitch she will
never take my house from me,
now get the fuck out of my car.

CRIPS: MY RETARDED SELF

You're shriveled up in that
chair again, drooling on yourself,
stuttering out your homework
on Dragon NaturallySpeaking.

Fuck you,
you faggot.
Do faggots
even fuck cripples?
I bet they don't.

Don't cry, you little bitch.
I can see you pretending to
cry. Did I ever tell you about
the time I saw you in the mirror
in high school?

The way your
knuckles rocked
made my stomach
turn.

 You had my Germs shirt on,
give it back to me!

I've got Skrewdriver on in the bathroom.
I'm doing Nazi salutes and jerking
off to thoughts of blond boys.

QUEERS: SEXY DREAMS

Kissing on you
as you felt up
my tits was so
fucking perfect.

You touched me
like my gimpy body
was soft, malleable
and valuable as gold

I could change from
boy to girl in seconds,
but the ache in my
 thighs lingered

until I woke up,
came on my sheets,
shuddered,
remembered.

REMINGTON

I'd been smoking weed and drinking
in Wyman Park all day with
crust punk kids almost twice
my age. In the grass, pants
around my ankles, I was a child,
I guess the grass was a child.

Before we knew it, it was night
we'd eaten every spore of shrooms.
My friends all walked away from me
and everything got really distant,
the grass was about to swallow me,
I started crawling, then crying,
my friend said, "Ty, are you ok?
You got like five feet in an hour."
they'd been there in front
of me, never left, just
stood up.

I cried, I touched
the grass, it felt like
skin, it was mine,
it was me, I was the grass,
and I stood up too.

CRIPS: SEX TALK

I fell in love
with a lot of
women, broke
up for reasons
that had nothing
to do with being blind,
broke some hearts,
you will too.

You can be with
any person,
man or woman
or whatever,
but don't accept
pity sex, ever.

I knew a few
blind guys in
 the '70s and '80s
who said they were
gay, I doubt they
really were,

I think they learned to
suck a good dick so they
wouldn't be alone. I
hope that's not what
you're thinking.

SISTER: SAVANNAH

Why was Ben so pissed off
about me smoking weed in
your living room? Doesn't he
get that I was having a spasm?

You're not yourself when
you're around him—sorry,
I'm not insulting him, just
saying he can be a bit of
a dick sometimes and you

let it slide, even say some
shit that makes you sound
like mom and dad. I just-
sorry again, I didn't mean
to say it like that.

Let's go for a walk outside,
the Spanish moss is so pretty
hanging from the trees that
you wouldn't even guess it was
a parasite. Dad said the street
smells like horse piss in summer
cuz of the carriages, poor horses.

You're coming back up for
my graduation, aren't you?

CRIPS: OLD COLLEGE TRY

Listen, kid, you gotta get out
on your own. If you don't do it
now, you might never
be able to. I'm serious.

The longer you wait to leave home,
the less likely it is that your
parents will ever see you as
a person, let alone an adult.

If you're scared to
wash dishes, fold clothes,
pay bills, you can do all that,
you've just never been expected to before.

You got into a state school and
nobody's tried to keep you out,
damn it, you go get
that education.

HOME: DREAM

In that cavernous room
the ceiling holds
painted limits of the skyway.
The chandelier is swinging like
a pendulum out of time.

T.V. screens are yammering,
over arguments about unpaid bills,
and talk about money and work,
at eight fuck you's per minute.

Stoned and napping
out by the pond
with the waterfall cascading down,
we think
this is a nice house.

II.

FIRST WEEK

In my room
There's a cold
off-white emptiness
and a shower
with a seat.

Nobody told me that
my groin muscle would
cramp every time I thought
it might be nice to fuck
a few of the girls or guys
in the hallway.

What if I can't last the whole week?
Wrapped in old bed sheets,
clothes strewn on the floor,
hamstrings seizing,
hips bucking, neck
bolted to the pillow,
drowning in tremors.

I should have left home
when I was fourteen.

BODY: POSTURE

Half-folded over,
knees locked.

Muscles stuck
like stones
in my neck,
feet stiff like
hockey pucks.

Fuck that paper,
I'm gonna do
laundry, then
go to bed.

CHILDHOOD: TRIKE

Dad clutched the
white rope tied
to my handlebars,
put blocks of wood
beneath my pedals.

Severed hamstrings
slowly cycling,
hand-me-down
helmet jostling
on my head.

I left that trike
covered in dust
next to paint cans
and plastic sleds.

The last ride,
I sucker punched
him in the gut.

HOME: PORCH

Back here again,
telling myself I'm
just visiting.

Heads of
black-eyed susans
bow to a pond
full of moss.

HOME: BEDROOM DOORWAY

Don't touch me,
I said don't
Fucking.
touch me.

Did you not hear me?
I don't want your cold calluses
anywhere near my neck.

Don't lick my neck,
it's weird.

Quit telling me I'm crazy.
I'm not, am I?
I don't want to do chin-ups.

Oh my G-d, I didn't mean
to hit you that hard, did
I knock your tooth loose?

Hurts, doesn't it?

QUEERS: CIS GIRLS

I've wanted to fuck you since we met,
but I don't want to use my dick,
like, if we fuck. Which we
don't have to.
We can just make out.

Wait, why are you putting
your hands there?
I thought you didn't want to fuck.
Are you sure you want
to do this right now?

You know what, forget it, it's
not important.
I really like that green dress
with the wooden beads on
the shoulder straps,
can I try it on?
Do you think I'd look hot in it?

It's totally cool
that you're a lesbian.
I guess I must be gay,
I do really like dudes,
but my life would
be easier if I were a girl,
you know?
I could date you.
I could wear dresses

like that green one, or that
orange one with the floral
print,

We can be friends,
right? Let's be friends.

MOTHER: CONTRACEPTION

Turn your music down, you
piece of shit, you fucking
waste of time and space,

You know I never wanted you,
it was his birthday,
I told him no, but he
went in anyway.

No one would believe me,
We were married, my last
pregnancy was terrible, I
almost died a few different
times. I was driving and
swerved off the road, I
don't remember anything
but waking up in a hospital bed.

I love you, I'm glad
to have you now.
Why don't you have a girlfriend?

You're straight, right?
Please tell me you're
straight. Whatever
you do, use protection.

LETTER TO SHAME

I felt you on the playground,
four years old, clutching the handles
on each side of my walker, wheels
bumping over woodchips. I fell face
first, got a mouthful of mulch.
My preschool teacher laughed,
the other kids around me started
laughing, too. All but this one girl,
who cried and I thought it was so
nice for her she had the luxury
of crying for someone else.

On the first day of kindergarten,
my parents wouldn't stop fighting,
we were running late, my father
scooped me up and ran me to his car.
My mother stood in the doorway
of our house, left breast hanging out
of her pajama top, middle finger
in the air, screaming,
"Fuck you, Bob! Fuck you!"

When my father's fist hit my
face at the first inkling of
girlhood, I named you the
blue dress in the closet and
promised I would leave you hanging.

One Halloween, when I was thirteen
I saw your face in the mirror.
My mother asked, "What do you want
to be this year?" I said, "A woman."
She laughed and told me we could go to
the Halloween store and pick up a
blonde wig and a styrofoam pair of
tits, they jostled when I walked.

A group of kids my age
said "what the hell are you?"
and "are your crutches
part of your costume?"
Someone's dad asked
why I wasn't wearing a costume,
told me I looked beautiful.
I told him I didn't feel
like wearing a costume this year,
but you were dripping from every
syllable in that sentence.

My mother shook me yesterday,
I came downstairs in my sister's
sundress, told her this was
me, she screamed, "You can't
do this to me!" I should've
cried, what was wrong
with me, I swear I felt
you there like I braced
myself for a slap in the
face, but I was disappointed.

QUEERS: ONE OF THE BOYS

I dragged my foot behind
the rest of the pack. I could
never lift the coffee table,
I could never hit the punching bag
hard enough. It always swung back
and hit me in the face,
I wanted to hit it so hard
it broke off of its chain.

"Do you get laid, bro?
Do you think lesbians are hot?
Stop being so fucking gay,
I bet you could get one of those
bitches you hang out with to fuck you."

When I wake up to wash the make-up
off my face, I remind myself
that seven shots of Kentucky Gentleman
will never put enough
hair on my chest for me not
to want to rip it out the next morning.

SISTER: BARCELONA

Look at those pigeons,
they're fighting for a
spot on that ledge,
that building must be
hundreds of years old.

God, this weed is
so good, can you
believe this breeze?

This is your city.
I can see why you'd
want to stay here.

SISTER: ZOLOFT

You pulled the nose
off my sculpture,
remember?

Remember
all those times
mom and dad
couldn't pick you up
from school,
so I had to?
Remember when we were
in a hit and run?

We both got hungry,
so we stopped at Wawa,
we couldn't park in
the handicap spot because
we didn't have your
sticker, so I ran in.

You yelled at me
for taking too long,
I was like,

"You walk in there
and buy food,
see how long that
takes you."

And then I hit the car
next to us when I pulled out.

I'd just gotten
my fucking
learners,
what did they
expect?

All my memories
from that time are
fuzzy, I don't think
I really needed
the meds I was on,
they made me
numb to everything–

By the way, are we on
for Parc Guell tomorrow?
It's gonna be a lot of walking
for you, but--

but what I
just said was coming
back so sharp–
Why was I the crazy one?

SISTER: QUEERS

It's gonna take some time
to wrap my head around
the fact that I might have
a sister, but I'll tell you
what, you can wear
all the clothes I left
at mom and dad's.

Every time I told
each of my boyfriends
that I was into girls,
They said, "not while
you're with me,"

You remember my friend
Marianne from high school?
I loved her, we almost dated.
I don't wanna know what
mom and dad said about us.

I don't know if I'm ready
to call you my sister,
but I'm fine with "they,"
and "sibling," if you say
that works for you.

AUNT: MANHATTAN BATHROOM

How was I supposed to know
you were coming into the ladies'
room? It didn't occur to me.

I just can't call you my niece,
I can try, I can see that it
hurts you, but it doesn't
make sense. To me, you'll
always be the smiling little
boy doing arts and crafts in the hospital.

Your parents don't understand,
but I'm sure they will, some day,
if you give them a chance.
We all love you, even if you don't
think so, my little Tyler-Wyler.

AUNT: LOW SUGAR

When you were a baby,
your mother was holding
you, she was passed out
in her rocking chair, I
unlocked the door as
she dropped you, you
cried. She was sweating
like a pig. Later that visit,

she threw dishes at my
head because I accidentally
broke a glass. Before you
or your sister were born,
when your parents were
first dating and I'd just
broken up with my fiancé,
my dad and I went on a
weekend ski trip with
them to Pennsylvania,

Pam got angry at Bobby,
started throwing pots
and pans, screaming
at the top of her lungs,

My dad looked at your dad,
said, "Bobby, listen to me, son,
you'd better not marry that woman."
I think he was right, you know?

AUNT: HOSPITAL

You brought popsicle sticks,
glitter glue, washable markers,
We made little houses or picture
frames, maybe both, can't remember,
nurses brought peach nectar,
dinosaur-shaped chicken nuggets,
Benadryl, morphine, sleep.

You held my hand,
stroked my knuckles,
looked at me, fading,
I wanted to get out
of that feshtinkina
place, after surgery
I wanted to go with
you to New York.

I couldn't tell you, but
when you weren't there,
I hated the hospital.
I wasn't a boy then, either.

HOME: ARCHITECT

Napoleon in hair plugs,
Bronx boy, spackle-stains
on jeans, sawdust on t-shirt,
nigger jokes, loud laughs,
stubby, calloused fingers,
gap-toothed, electric blue-green
eyes like whirlpools,
he crushed big screen TVs
and home theater seats
under mountains of debt,
smoked weed out of
test tubes and PVC pipes.

He laid the tile all himself,
it was years before he fixed
the sink. He moved us in
months before we had
running water, his
house, his model,
his show-and-tell
his wife, his children,
his awards, his property,
he didn't have any friends,
just guys he played tennis
with, and kids from the old neighborhood
who got richer than he did, he couldn't
stand it. Show-off, know-it-all, asshole,
wife-beater, kid-diddler, "Stop it with
the name calling," he said,

"Look at the ramp in the garage
and the railings in the bathrooms,
I designed and built this house for you."

MOTHER: ORANGE JUICE

Let the citrus stain my teeth,
give me canker sores that swirl
like white galaxies on my lower lip

Give it to in me sippy cups
in the car on the way to school
You're low, you know you need
to drink it more than I do, so
just fucking drink it!

I don't want it flavored with
pineapple, mango, or tangerine.
I want it with a black, blue,
white, and green layer
of mold on the bottom,
leave it in the fridge for months, I'll
taste it to see if it's good enough for you.

MOTHER: TALK THERAPY

I could have walked to her room
with a kitchen knife
and slit her wrists so easily,
but I brought her testing kit instead and
placed her bloody finger on the strip,
it was 17, do you know what a 17 blood
sugar looks like?

She groaned, she couldn't speak, if she dipped
below double digits, she would have died,
I slid glucose tablets into her open mouth,
I should have called an ambulance, she hated
ambulances. When she came to, she bit me.

School ended at 3:30 and I
remember waiting til 5:30, she'd pick me up with 30
blood sugar, close her eyes on the road and I would
pray for a car crash. I shook her awake, I could've
smashed her face into the steering wheel,
what the hell was wrong with me?

I was warming up her dinner,
wiping the sweat from her forehead, watching
television, getting ready for synagogue,
staring at the clock while the kids around
me played wheelchair basketball,
there was no escape for me,

I waited for thunderstorms to go out
and catch raindrops on my tongue,
all I wanted was a bad cold, pneumonia,
or something that would kill me.

MOTHER: MIRROR

Do you see through my stubble?
Do you forgive my eyebrows?
My shaking hands would paint my eyelids,
but they've been balled up in fists all day.

I've been drinking with frat boys,
covering rusted crutch cuffs
with duct tape, not making
excuses after I pass out at 5 a.m.

Do you know how you
made me feel?
I never cut my wrists,
I was smarter than to
give my teachers, doctors,
aides, and physical therapists,
a peek at the color of my blood.

I'm starting to look more like
you as my hair grows out.
At least I don't look like him.

MOTHER: SEE YOU NEVER

I never touched you like that,
at least not that I can remember,
I didn't know what I was doing,
I don't know what I was thinking.

I never put my mouth on you,
that's a fucking lie. If I did,
I had a low blood sugar,
I get horny when I have
low blood sugars.

I guess I would do that to any
male. You can't tell me you're
not male, you'll always be
male to me. I don't care if
you wear a dress.

You'll be fine, goddamnit.
I'm still your mother, right?

CHILDHOOD: SWEET DREAMS

When the light switches were talking
to the stuffed animals at the top of the bookshelf,
she flooded me in pages of "Cat in the Hat,"
mowed me down like The Onceler, and stole all
the pancakes from my favorite pig.

"Turn off the Nintendo,
We couldn't eat for a week after we
got you that. It's all your fault.
I love you, sweetie pie. "

III.

MOTHER'S DAY

I don't want to watch "Annie Hall," with you,
I don't want to trace the thickness of the veins on your
   knuckles,
I'm not making you a card,
I'm not bringing you orange juice,
Forget about the coffee in the microwave.
You are a mess of green sheets and gold-plated bed posts,
you had ten gray pubic hairs when you were fifty-two,
I can still feel your fingers on my asscheek, I don't want
   to smoke pot
with you, you are my never, my worst, my not in a
   million fucking years,
you are the ghost of your mother,
I prayed to gods I didn't believe in for you,
I wanted to believe in you, I never want to be
alone with you, I don't belong to you,
you're wrong, leave me alone!

Can we go someplace other than IHOP, anywhere but
   IHOP,
I hate the way I've watched him squeeze your ass, force
   your lips against his,
here I am, still not yours, still not your baby, still not
   your man,
I'm sweating from the roofbeams of
our unfinished house,
I am lost in Laurel with you again, or are we in Columbia?
Do you know where we are? Mom, where are we? Mom,

wake up, don't make me call 911. Dad is gonna be so
    pissed at me,
talk to me, say something, I don't want to force
another melted butterscotch down your throat, we're in
the middle of DC, did you take a wrong turn somewhere?
Bonnie called and said you missed
your 8:30 tennis game this morning;
I told her you were sick. I'm not about to make a scene,
I promise, just get your prescription filled so we can
go to Burger King and take care of your blood sugar.
You fucked everything up, I fucked everything up, fuck
    you,
you're the only person who makes me wish I'd never
    been born.

FATHER'S DAY

I don't want to go to Camden Yards with you,
I don't want to smoke pot with you,
I'm not making you a card,
I'm not picking up the tennis racket
I'm not getting into the wheelchair,
and for the last time, I don't want to fuck my physical
    therapist,
You said, "you need to find a hot woman who inspires
    you to do
your exercises. If you can stretch better, you can fuck
    better, That's a fact."
You bent mom over her desk and spanked her
for not knowing where the Baltimore County Line was,
fuck you motherfucker,

my nightmares are of crawling into bed with you,
your head comes off and sprouts spider legs,
I remember the ways you touched me in the
    spongebaths after surgery,
there were times I would ask you to kiss me,
I didn't mean it, you dryhumped me by the old toybox,
the one with the naked doll sticking out of it,
I'm scared and I don't want to be tickled, I'm gonna pee
    my pants, stop, it hurts, game
over, I don't want to play tennis with you,
did you mean for that first serve to hit me, I don't want
    to know,
I don't want to be a part of this,

I am sweating from the roofbeams of
our unfinished house,
you ran your fingers through my hair and said,
"To think she wanted me to wear a condom. I'm glad I
went in anyway. It's not rape if you're married, tyboy."
You scare me as much I scare myself, you scare me more
    than she does,
more than the time she wrapped her hands around my
    neck,
I called you crying, you hung up on me,
you are fucking dead to me.

MERMAID

Losing gravity in the Chesapeake,
grooved leg bones slowly fusing,
skin forming into scales.

Wet, wavy hair streaking
across my shoulders,
clamshell bra falling off.

Face in the water,
not trying to drown
for once,
my bones don't
click anymore, I'm not
wading or standing
in the water like a
crane, I'm not gasping,
I'm swimming away.

IV.

BODY: RABBIT HOLE

One pill makes
your breasts bigger,
One pill makes
your testes smaller,
yellow-orange disk,
baby blue tear drop,
tiny little thing,
every twelve hours.

Skin will soften,
voice will not,
write "beautiful,"
in lipstick across
chest to remind
yourself.
This is beginning
& no turning back.

HOME: MOVING

We're putting the house on the market,
I know what it was like when
my mother threw out all my stuff,
I will get yours to you somehow,
when my parents moved I was heartbroken,
I lived with them until I was twenty-five,
I took my chinning bar down
from your bedroom doorway, I
fixed the frame, the door locks now,
we are leaving, we are packing up
your room, is there anything you want from it?

We're taking the house off the market.
I have copies of your passport and your Social Security
card, these are not things you should leave with me. Why
don't you talk to me? I miss you, you're making
your mother cry. Is that what you want?

Why didn't you come home for Thanksgiving?
It's been a year. We bought tofurkey for you,
it's still in the freezer, I can get it to you,
we bought you Hanukah presents,
we bought you textbooks for next year,
we'll pay your tuition, go back to school,
grandma will pay your tuition, you can get
money from FAFSA, we would like
to see you in school, weren't there good times?
You think you were neglected, so sue me, I had jobsites

and tennis games, I couldn't always be there, your
mother's fucking crazy, what can I say?

We are putting the house on the market again,
we will soon, once we have cleaned everything out. I
won't throw away your CDs and books,
email me to say you will not write "Return to Sender,"
and they will be in the mail tomorrow,
do you want your old VHS tapes?

You have so many things that we bought
for you over the years, don't you appreciate
that? There are still boxes in the attic
from when we moved in, I'll see if anything up there
belongs to you, we are selling the house, I can
give you some pot, your mother found a
drawing you did when you were six, can we
please keep that? Don't worry,
we are taking everything with us to the next house.

MOTHER: RETURN TO SENDER

Two-hundred and ten dollars for my
twenty-first birthday and all the legal medical
marijuana in the world couldn't make me forgive you.

Why do I have to remember
the azaleas in our front yard, your yellow sundress,
and me, little, plump, and blonde
I wasn't afraid of you that day;
I was smiling, you held me up,
I was picking flowers, sticking them in your hair.

Part of me wants you to leave Bob,
have your own life, do what you want.

All I ever say to you is
RETURN TO SENDER.
and hope the ink bleeds through
the envelope. I've burned and
torn so many letters, but they kept
coming, do you get the message now?

Bob's dead to me, but you aren't,
It's not like I want to see you,
or will be with you when you die,
It's just, for better or worse,
I guess you're alive.

MOTHER: HOME

It's your fault she left, Bob.
She won't talk to us because
you can't accept her, you could
never leave her the fuck alone.

Let her do what she wants,
Isn't that what you're supposed to
do as a parent? You don't get it.

Not everyone gets to
live with mommy and
daddy until mommy
guilts their pregnant
cousin into finding
them an apartment
in a state they've
never been to.

He–I mean she
is a brilliant kid,
She'll be fine,
she might even
come around one day.

HOME: MOTHER

It's my fault?
fuck you, Pam,
it's your fault.

You never took care of
him, he hates you.

He's my only son.
You don't get it,
he needs us.

It's fucking sad that
you had your own
apartment at 17,
your parents were
too drunk to love you.

I'm worried about him,
I'm going down there.

QUEERS: WHY WE BUY BLACK MARKERS

Get the fuck away from our house,
Ty doesn't want to see you at all,
she knows what's good for her,
so just fucking leave already.

I don't blame her one bit,
She flat out hates you, dude,
what's not to get?

She kept her blinds shut
for two months after the
last time you came by uninvited,
we lock all of our windows now,
can't you take a hint?

You want a relationship with her
and you can't even get her pronouns
right? Who are you to ask
if my parents call me she all the time?
You don't know me, motherfucker.

For all you know, I might not
even know my dad and I
might be glad that I don't.

AUNT: GUILT TRIP

Your parents are worried about you.
Why wouldn't they be?
I mean, you never talk to them,
you never talk to me. They're
your parents, of course they love you.
They never told me that you
told them to stop talking to you.
Why would you do that to them?

I know your dad can be
horrible sometimes, he's
my baby brother, so I always
gave him a talking to, I don't
know where he got it from,
your mother's parents were
fucked up, maybe he got it from her.

It drove him crazy
when she was in low sugar.
but you had it so much better
than so many other kids. Let
me tell you, your mother
and father are always going
to be your mother and father.

QUEERS: FUCK THIS

I am alone in life.
My raised voice resounds
off of floor tiles.
I ain't nothin' better
or worse than you.

Who can I trust?
They feel like breasts
to me now. I've never
been so happy. This
body might know what it wants.

I want all of you to want all of me,
of course you're not going to, nobody
does. I want to turn all of you down.

QUEERS: CRIPS

I'm sorry,
the stairs don't
have a handrail.

I have a couch
you can crash on,
but the only
bathroom's upstairs,
is that okay?

I feel like
a bad activist,
I mean, a bad friend.

I haven't hung out
with many disabled
people before, is
that the right term?

Would you feel
comfortable sharing
my bed tonight?

I can help you
up the steps
if you need.

It's ok if not,
I just want you
to feel safe here.

CRIPS: QUEERS

I've fucked a lot
of able-bodied queers.
They don't want
to pity you,

but their first
time with a
disabled person
is probably gonna
be with you, so

you gotta give
them a chance
to unlearn all the
bullshit; it can
take years, but most
of them won't, not even
the good ones.

My partner
and I dated for
three years,
they'd always say,

"You go through so much,
babe, I can't even imagine."

Once, I said,
 "Shut up, you don't

have to imagine, do you?
You either need to help
me, or get the fuck out of my way."

QUEERS: TRANS GIRLS

Come over, let's
smoke some weed
or drink some wine,
I could show you
some of my poems.

My tits are burning
like a motherfucker.
I feel like there should be
ash dripping from
my nipples.

I need someone to touch them.
Maybe we can do that for
each other. Kiss me, it's ok.

Wait, why would you ask me
which bathroom I use?
What the hell does that mean?

I'm not more of a woman than you are.
You've been on hormones longer
and it's not a competition anyway.
Look at you, you're gorgeous, I swear.

I don't care that you were an asshole
to girls before you transitioned,
I mean, I care. it's fucked.

Why would you tell me that
in the middle of making out?

No, I don't want to suck on your tits
and I don't want you to suck on mine.
I'm sorry, I really am.

QUEERS: I UNDERSTAND

I always wanted to be the last friend standing,
to stop you from killing yourself
like you said you were going to,
tell you I believed you when no one did.

I am holding your clammy hands in your dim bedroom,
while you talk shit on our entire circle of friends,
you say they're all out to get you, but if I say they
aren't, I'm out to get you too, and maybe I am, but
all I want is for you to tell me you don't hate me.

Stop texting me at four in the morning
every goddamn day, some people need to sleep,
talk to your therapist about your flashbacks, not me.
You want me to feel bad for you, well, I do,
I'll cook you dinner if you promise not to berate me.

I told you that broken glass was hard for me to deal with
and you kept breaking mason jars,
I asked you to stop being so nonchalant about suicide,
everyone else told me to let you go,
I get where they're coming from.

It hurts like hell, but I don't need you.
Help yourself, take some fucking responsibility!

QUEERS: HOW NIGHT EATS MORNING

Woke up hungover and pissed off,
empathy and apathy sloshing in my gallbladder,
I love waking up to sunlight, though,
my room floods every time it rains.
two weeks later, I smell mold on my favorite pair of jeans.
We might need to feed those blackened banana peels to
    the rat-like
sponges of lint on the floor.

I'm cleaning cat litter, I'm cooking with cumin,
turmeric, and cayenne pepper, are you hungry?

QUEERS: SLEEP WITH ME

I have been dating myself for the past year;
I need to see other people,
the only thing I can do is ask if, maybe,
you want to share my bed for the night.

I only just worked up the guts to tell you
I like you and now you're saying you like me too,
some nights I try to masturbate and end up crying,
I feel like

I can never do anything right;
My nipples are sensitive, my leg muscles are stiff,
I realize none of this sounds like "I want you,"
I am still learning that sexual abuse isn't sex,
I don't even drink coffee,
but I love it when you're sitting across from me.

Let's just sit and let the joint smoke slide down our
    throats.

QUEERS: THE SUMMER

We killed that bottle of white
wine last night, I don't know
if you caught your bus.

The clove ashes on my dress
are so pretty, I don't even
want to brush them off. Let me crawl up
to Boston and
wrap my arms
around you, so
we can have more
days full of
song and smoke.

BACK TO SLEEP

I dreamed I was caressing
my friend.

accidently
kissed her lips
squeezed her hand,
then kissed it.

I let her
wake me up
to nothing.

ODE TO MY BOY JEANS

I wanna throw these out, but
I have nothing else to wear.

I can't shake the feeling that I'm wearing
a dead kid's clothes; that he was a ghost
who passed through the lives of people
I loved and lied about me. Some fucking ghost!
Always slipping on the floor at Sidebar,
it was sticky and soaked with beer, still is,
I can't remember when I washed them last,

I really should put them in the laundry and
give them to some trans guy I know,
they're all my height. There's a clothing
swap next week, I remember how happy I
was when I got all those dresses and skirts.

Damn it, this reminds me of
when I had blue hair and a beard,
can't believe how stupid I looked then
the hair dye stained the back of my
ears and neck for a week,
there's still a bleach stain on these jeans,
and of course they smell like weed,
who the hell do you think you're talking to?

I feel like I'm fifteen again,
I want blunts, and 40s of malt liquor.
No one calls me they anymore, I miss that.

I want a mirror that shows the boy and the girl
I've been holding hands, I ought
to wear this pair more often,
I want the kisses I was too scared to ask for
and I guess I'm keeping these jeans.

BODY: MY HIPS

My hips are tiny, not what
you'd call birthing hips.
They shake, not always on the
dance floor. Left bone
coming out of its socket
like a cue ball. There is a
dance in the swaying of
my gait, one foot sideways
in front of the other.

I like to trace the scar
on my left hip, naked, alone,
standing in front of the shower,
trying not to lock my knees,
I always feel like I'm gonna fall,
damn wobbly hips, always crooked.

I'm sorry I ever cursed them,
I've cried into them, if we went
through another surgery
I think I'd get up with them and
re-learn how to walk.

SISTER: BATON ROUGE

I.
Look, Ty, I don't think
it's the best idea for you
to wear a dress where
we're going. There are
people who could hurt
you here, you know?

II.
I don't need your permission,
Jamie, I'm wearing a dress.
It's 80 degrees outside anyway,
What the hell's the matter with you?

III.
I heard about two gay guys
who got their heads
bashed in a couple of
weeks ago, I don't
want that to happen to you.

IV.
Bullshit, why should I
closet myself here and
prance around DC in a
dress? That's a slap

in the face to the
trans women who live here.

V.
I'm worried, asshole,
I'm not the transphobic
one here, you've never
really been around these
people, it's different down here.

VI.
This isn't about going to Lafayette, is it?
You're uncomfortable with me right now.

VII.
I don't like how you
don't even give me
a chance to get it right.

There's a difference between
lending your brother women's clothes
and accepting that you have a sister.

You got off the train,
we went to my friend's
party, I said, "we," you
corrected me to, "she,"

VIII.
I wasn't talking about gender,
I was talking about us.

IX.
Excuse me?
Can we not do this right now?

X.
Sure, fine, whatever.
We'll talk later.

XI.
Look at us, drunk, lying
on a blanket in a swamp,
everything around us is
such a vibrant shade of green,
don't you think?

XII.
Yeah, except the mud.
Listen, Jamie, are you
happy here?

XIII.
Yeah, what do you mean?
It's not the greatest here,

but I manage, you know,
I've got friends, the program's
okay, I make enough to live on,
barely, but I do.

XIV.
Should I be here with you?
Like, was this trip a good idea?

XV.
Oh, honey, don't say that
I don't know, I feel like
my friends like you better
than they like me, and you're
not as appreciative as I'd like you to be.

XVI.
Where did that come from?
You sound like you've got
some shit you should work out.

XVII.
Why don't you work your own shit out?
You got so emotional when I told you
to shave, I don't think that's healthy.
You're too reactive these days.
You're gonna have to learn to deal
with the shit people say to you.

XVIII.
Like I don't get enough of that
from the world around me!
You don't get to comment
on my body. How would
you feel if hair grew on your face?

I'm a woman, too, for fuck's sake.

AUNT: RIVERDALE

I hate New York,
at least, I hate the
Bronx. If not the
Bronx, I hate the
Hudson, the Henry
Hudson pkwy to
be specific, the river's
never done me wrong.

One time, I was coming
in on the Jersey Turnpike
with my dad, smoking
a bowl, we passed
a woman whiter
than a ghost with
her head splattered
red through her sunroof,
before I knew it, it was
night and we were
speeding through
the EZ Pass lane,
the city spread out
around us like a
shimmering cancer.

For the first ten years of my life
all I saw of New York was your apartment
in Riverdale, you and my dad fought
like kids again,

You watched him hit me,
you watched him hit my mother,
you said you never saw him hit Jamie.

I know you're afraid of the subway,
I know not all of the stations are
accessible, but I'll be fine. The
express bus high-tails it through
Harlem to get the old white Jews
safely to Manhattan. If you insist
on driving me, take me down to

The Lower East Side, take the
FDR Drive. You want to do something
together? let's go to the Museum
of Natural History, like we did
when I was ten. We can stop
and get a knish, but after that,
I don't need you; I have friends here.

MOTHER: ANY DAY

Even though you hate me,
I love you and
am very proud of you.
whatever you choose is
well-thought and admired
by many.
No more correspondence,
I promise.

SISTERHOOD

I'm sorry I scribbled in pencil on your canvas,
I was six. I'm sorry mom screamed and
ordered you to hit me, I forgive you.
I'm sorry you couldn't get us out of there. I'm sorry
for stealing your walkman and all your favorite CD's,
well, maybe not sorry as much as thanks.

We were only children, nine years apart,
at the same time, we were never children.
You were four, but you knew Pam wasn't breathing
You called 911, said, "My mommy's
dead, my mommy's dead."
I made the same kinds of calls,
Were we more afraid of being
locked out of the house or into it?

I hit puberty, told you I liked boys but
I was also a lesbian, you said, "Honey,
lesbians don't want any part of you,
especially not that part of you,"
I thought maybe you'd understand me.

I always wished I could draw like you,
learn to sculpt and paint, learn lithography and
photography and smell the darkroom
chemicals and keep a messy studio
where I hung wooden parrots,
and Christmas lights.

Would you take
another look at my sketchbook?
Dad told me it was primitive,
I'm a bad artist, every line
I draw has bumps, curves,
Divots, swerves, and slopes
like the streets of Providence,

I'll always be walking the streets of Gracia with you,
looking out for graffiti that says, "Fuck the Police,"
and means it. When you came home from Birthright
I put a glass to my lips before we said the Kiddush
and you shouted, you startled me, I spilled grape
juice all over the tablecloth and you told me
stories of the IDF soldiers you met, they were
just building the wall then and now
we agree that Gaza is an open-air prison.

I would skip a month's rent to see you,
I sat twenty-seven hours on a
train to Baton Rouge and twenty-seven hours
back to DC and I wanted to sleep til Baltimore,
but they wouldn't let me. I would hitchhike to
you if I had to, I'd traverse this country's gas
stations and rest stops.

Thank you for walking out in front of me from that
convenience store women's room in Louisiana, I
        needed that.

Do you know easy it would be for us to hate each
other?

We could hang up the phone and let the years balloon
out with animosity, we could blame each other
for so many of our own mistakes, we could
stop laughing at our inside jokes
and start breaking down at the sound
of each others' names, smoke
would come out of our ears like in forties cartoons,
you didn't have to give me my favorite dresses,
you didn't have to help me put on my shoes, but you did,
you're not here to save me or raise me,
we're two women with more than trauma in common.
This is sisterhood.

SMALLTIMORE

I sat on my porch,
walked to Ottobar to
meet a friend for drinks.

We danced and kissed
I walked back
to my house at 2am
tipsy, tired, and sore.

Ran into my cute neighbor,
made plans for next Saturday,
climbed the steps to my room,
scooped cat litter, fell asleep
with my clothes on, woke up
at sunrise, took them off,
and went back to bed.

ACKNOWLEDGEMENTS

Jamie Kutner, Arti Malhotra, Ginger Coyote, Cat Fitzpatrick, Tom Legér, Bonnie Boto, Colleen Jordan, Jay Imbrenda, Mike Bullis, Johnna Schmidt, Zein El-Amine, Vivienne Salgado, Jim Sullivan, Regie Cabico, Natalie E. Illum, Danielle Evennou, Kris Gebhard, Gowri K, Sarah D. Lawson, Dane Edidi, Monica Stevens, Ryka Aoki, Emma Caterine, Venus Hinyard, Alain Ginsberg, Imogen Binnie, Casey Plett, Sybil Lamb, Penny Rimbaud, Charles Theonia, Lilith Latini, Kool Aid, Dirk, Sue Werner, Spoonboy, Foster Gettys, Jenna Brager, Grey Read, Rahne Alexander, the Robinson family, Aaron Burgess, Laurie Gwen Shapiro, Bryanna Jenkins, Kay Ulanday Barrett, J Mase III, Vita E, other people in my life that I'm forgetting (I know, I'm a jerk, sorry) Lucille Clifton, Gwendolyn Brooks, Lucia Sánchez Saornil, Emma Goldman, Rosa Luxemburg, Patricia Smith, Poly Styrene, Jayne County, Marsha P. Johnson, Sylvia Rivera, Chelsea Manning.

ABOUT THE AUTHOR

Tyler Vile is a poet, performer, and activist from Baltimore, MD who has had her work featured in publications like in *Gadfly, Bluestockings Magazine, Trans Poets Will Burn Your House Down*, and *The Round Up Writers' Zine*. She performs regularly in the Baltimore-DC area, including at DC's Sparkle Queer Open Mic and Capturing Fire. She has written for *Punk Globe Magazine* since 2007 and is featured in *The Best of Punk Globe* anthology. Her poetry zine, *Hasidic Witch Murderer*, is available by request. *Never Coming Home* is her first full-length book. Her favorite Baltimore past-times are getting hiccups from Natty Boh and side-eying yuppies. One day, she will become the world's greatest transsexual yenta.

ABOUT HELIOTROPE

Heliotrope is a dedicated series of poetry books by transgender authors. We value writing which is sincere, direct, self-aware, and which tells a story (or several). The poetry we publish is a challenge. It's a tool, but it's also a dare to use that tool: to talk more; to think harder; to believe in yourself *and* question yourself; maybe even to write some poems of your own.

In this first series, Heliotrope will publish books by Lilith Latini, Charles Theonia, Tyler Vile and Kay Ulanday Barrett.

Heliotrope is an imprint of Topside Press and is edited by Cat Fitzpatrick. Cat teaches literature at Rutgers University - Newark and organizes the Trans Poets Workshop NYC.

Poets are welcome to join the Trans Poets Workshop- more information at transpoets.com

Submissions of poetry manuscripts are welcome year-round at topsidepress.com